CALVIN MILLER

THE UNSINKABLE ROCK

The Story of Simon Peter in Rhyme

Illustrated by Marc Harrison

THOMAS NELSON PUBLISHERS
NASHVILLE

Long, long ago,
When Peter was a little boy,
He used to watch the restless sea,
And throw in rocks to hear them fall,
So plunking and so splashingly.
The rocks he threw would gurgle down
And sink with chug-a-lugging sounds.

Published in Nashville, Tennessee, by Thomas
Nelson, Inc., and distributed in Canada by Law-
son Falle, Ltd., Cambridge, Ontario.

ISBN 0-8407-6722-6   1 2 3 4—90 89 88 87

I'm quite a bit like Peter, too.
I like to throw in rocks, don't you?
Most every rock will sink, it's true.
But read this story if you think
That every rock will simply sink.

Back when Peter threw those rocks,
No one had names like me and you—
Names like Bob or Lora Lee
Or Bill or Phil or Tom or Sue!
Jesus' friends had longer names,
Like Matthew and Bartholomew.

Back then their names were long enough
To tell where they were from, it's true,
Like Lazarus of Bethany
By Olivet! Wow! Goodness! Whew!

Now Peter who was Jesus' friend
Grew up beside a silver sea.
No one called him Peter till
He was well past twenty-three.
And it wasn't Peter's mom or dad
From whom the name of Peter came.
No! Someone very special gave
Peter such a special name.

Can you guess who? One guess or two?
Two guesses, maybe even three?
If it wasn't Peter's mom,
Then whoever could it be?
His mother named him Simon of
Capernaum beside the sea.
That's quite a name!
Don't you agree?
(By the way that silver sea
Was called the Sea of Galilee.)

Well, Simon of Capernaum
Grew up. And then eventually
He bought himself a boat or two
And fished a lot on Galilee.

One day he dragged his boat ashore
To patch a soggy fishing net.
When suddenly he raised his eyes,
And wow, can you guess who he met?
Well! Can you guess? You're right! They met
And briskly hugged there in the sun—
"I'm Jesus Christ of Nazareth!"
"I'm Simon of Capernaum!"

Then Jesus spoke there by the dock.
"From now on, Simon, you're the Rock!
The Rock, I say, will be your name."
(Now Peter is the word for rock
In the language Jesus talked.)

Jesus then went on to say,
"You're a rock so very strong
I'm going to build My church upon
Your life and faith. And then you'll be
The Rock that holds My glorious church
Through time and all eternity."

"I'm Peter, but I'm still the same!
I simply have a brand new name.
This has been some day and how!
This morning I was Simon, but . . .
Look at me! I'm Peter now!"

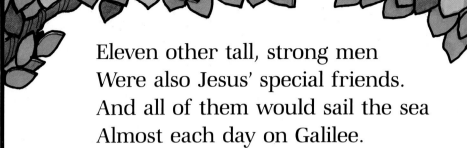

Eleven other tall, strong men
Were also Jesus' special friends.
And all of them would sail the sea
Almost each day on Galilee.

It happened on a lovely day
When Jesus stayed behind to pray.
His twelve disciples sailed away,
But the sun did not stay warm.

The clouds rolled in and then a storm.
The thunder roared. The rain poured down.
The men cried, "Jesus help! We'll drown!"
But Jesus wasn't on the boat,
Which lurched and barely stayed afloat.

Jesus was kneeling on the ground.
Still in His mind He heard the sound
Of His friends crying they would drown
Because the sea was upside down!

He knew He must go to His friends
But had no boat to get to them.
So He decided there and then
He'd walk across the sea to them.

Sound impossible to you?
It's not all that hard to do—
If you were just the Son of God.
You could step out on any sea.
Just don't look down! Now that's the key!
Just right foot, left foot, one, two, three!

So Jesus walked out steppingly.
Right foot, left . . . Across the sea!
He saw His friends! And as they stared
Jesus saw those men were scared!

Know what scared His friends the most?
They thought that Jesus was a ghost.
I guess the lightning of the night
Made His robe look ghostly-bright
And gave His friends an awful fright.

When James and John Bar Zebedee
(Two of His friends from Galilee)
Saw Him standing on the sea,
They cried in fear, "What shall we do?"
"Hey, look at this, Bartholomew!"
Just then the fiery lightning flashed!
Bartholomew saw Jesus, too.
Another friend cried, "Help! Oh, whew!
Good grief, a ghost! What will we do?"

"Fear not . . . It's Me," was Jesus' plea,
"I'm walking to you on the sea."

"Oh, wow!" cried Peter, "If it's You,
I'd like to walk on water, too."

"Come on then, Peter; it's like the ground.
It's easy if you don't look down.
Just keep your eyes glued hard to Me,
You'll find it's easy as can be."

Peter jumped down on the sea.
He thought he'd sink in to his knees,
But boy, was he surprised and pleased.
And he just stood there as he grinned!
"Jesus, You are such a friend."

Peter then felt simply grand
That he could look at Christ and stand,
Or walk, or skip, as though he planned
A shopping trip on solid land!

Walking on the sea was fun!
And Peter knew it was God's Son
Who helped him get the walking done.
But Peter then became so proud
He very proudly said out loud,
"Gee! I can do this all alone!"

He took his eyes off Christ . . . and well
He took one step and promptly fell.
The cold sea came up to his knees

And then his waist. He felt he'd freeze.
And as he tried to swim and grapple,
Water reached his Adam's apple.
And then it covered up his head.
He thought for sure he'd soon be dead.
"Help . . . Lord . . . Please help.
I've really flubbed.
Help, Jesus . . . help! Save me!
Glub! Glub!"

And Jesus reaching in the sea,
Pulled Peter back up on his feet,
And said, "Please, Rock, have faith in Me!
Why did you doubt? Believe, you'll see!"

The Rock then walked and stayed afloat
Till both of them got to the boat.
A friend who met them at the brink
Said "Peter, you're the rock! Just think
God made one Rock that couldn't sink."

And this just proves
what you can do
If you have faith in Jesus, too.
You may never walk the sea,
But be the best kid you can be.
You can do more than you think.
Ask the Rock that couldn't sink.